LET'S SMILE TOGETHER :)

ONE STEP TOWARDS HAPPY LIFE

NK KRISHNA

ISBN 979-888521891-7

Contents

Let's Smile Together :)

A Step towards Happy life..

Nk Krishna

FOUNDER OF TEC & ENTREPRENEUR

CHAPTER ONE

FINANCIAL HEARTBEAT

Disclaimer:- I am no financial expert or coach but I have been managing my finance pretty decent for the past 6.5 years.

1* Have emergency funds saving account:- I am putting my income in one of my savings accounts, use this only in case of a dire emergency, if this is hard get rid of its debit card & uninstall an app from the phone. this should be independent of a mutual fund, stocks & fd.

2*NO EMIs for liabilities:- this includes cars, expensive gadgets, appliances etc, buy those only when you can afford them in full cash.

3* ALWAYS look for assets, not for liabilities.

4* DON'T spend too much on your marriage:- I have seen people spending their 10 years of savings on marriage (* personally I am thinking to donate /building a school for studiousness near my farmhouse "Shadi ki nishani :)")

5. When you are tempted to buy things, ask yourself these questions.

Do I need this? Really? How extent?

Do I need this right now?

Can I buy this in future?

Is it worth buying it now at this price?

After these still you feel to buy it, don't buy blindly.

Search for the best price.

Go for DESIDIME .

Search if there are any offers or coupons I can apply.

There is a quote.

You will never get rich by earning more but you will get rich by saving more.

6. Use of credit card very judiciously:- pay the due on-time credit card debt, if unpaid can easily f**ck your civil score as well as peace of mind.

7. LEARN from others:- Don't make all the mistakes yourself. no one has time, it's a lot cheaper & rewarding.

8. PATH TO financial path:-

There are 3 types of people.

sidewalk:- These are people who earn money and do not invest it anywhere. The incoming income is equal to the expenditure. So, they have no money to save. In the end, they become broke. Examples include KBC winners (10 million), who did not invest the money anywhere, now they are bankrupt.

slow lane:- These people invest money in Mutual Funds or FD's or stocks. They work for 25–30 years, save money and then have a happy retired life. These include most of the middle-class people.

fast lane:- These are the people who add value to other people's lives. This is the fastest way to reach financial independence. You can not reach financial independence by just adding value to your life. You have to do something that adds value to other people's lives. Take an example, Mark Zuckerberg, Elon Musk, Ambani, Tata or not so famous ones like the youtube stars like Siraj Raval, Stand up comedians etc. All these people are doing something that affects not just themselves but a large circle.

So, if you want to reach your goal of financial freedom, add value to other people's lives.

9. Buy a life insurance:- I know, life insurances are trap and we don't get much returns etc., but go ahead and buy one. I know we are still young and perfectly in good health but if I die in a accident tomorrow, I want my family to be covered.

10. Last but not least, your health & mental peace are biggest assets . never compromise with your health for job just because of you're getting good salary (*I resigned a few jobs for this)

BONOUS TIPS:-

Be careful while shopping online. Do not run behind offers.Below story will teach you a lesson:

Situation 1:

It is late night and you are walking home from office after a long and tiring day.

You are thirsty but your water bottle is empty. Your house is still far and you know that if you don't drink water soon, you will not be able to walk.

Suddenly, you see an open shop in the distance. A convenience store!

You approach the owner and ask for a bottle of water.

He hands over a bottle of water to you

You are delighted to hold the bottle in your hand and a sense of happiness surrounds you.

You check the bottle for the MRP indication. It is Rs.10, you remove the cash and hand it over to the owner.

The owner looks at you and says "The price will be Rs. 20"

You look at him in disbelief. You know your legal rights and that the owner is unethical and wrong. There is no way out at the moment, and you eventually pay him Rs.20.

Situation 2:

It is again late night and you are walking home after a tiring day. You feel thirsty but you remember you have ample water with you.

So you remove your water bottle, quench your thirst and continue your journey home.

On the way, as you pass by a convenience store, the owner approaches you and says, "Today, we have an irresistible offer and you just cannot miss it. A water bottle of MRP Rs.10 is available at Re.1 only!!! Hurry up, offer expires midnight!"

You look at him, smile and walk away.

So what do we learn?

The principle is simple;

If there is a genuine need, it is okay to pay even Rs.20 for a thing costing Rs.10

but

if there is no need, it is not okay to pay even Re.1 for a thing costing Rs.10, no matter how good the offer seems!

This is such a basic principle that we always tend to ignore it.

So before you proceed to pounce on that next great online offer before it expires, ask yourself – "Do I really need this?"

This always helps me keep things in perspective while purchasing anything and is undoubtedly the most valuable financial advice that I have ever received.

CHAPTER TWO

Before reading this. let me tell you one thing.

"NO MATTER HOW MANY BOOKS OR BLOGS YOU READ OR VIDEOS YOU WATCH ON SELF-IMPROVEMENT, IF YOU DON'T TAKE ACTION THEN IT IS USELESS"

1* Never ever depend upon a single income. so, start looking for 2nd income from today. because you would never know when would your company stop loving you.

2* It would be awesome to not peep into someone's problem/ life. become selfish & utilise your time to upgrade yourself.

3* Always try to appreciate the good things & make sure that should be genuine, not cheesy. because good vibes attract good vibes. Add this habit.

4* Never lose your virginity to a prostitute, I repeat, never ever lose virginity to a prostitute.

5* Give equal importance to your work & personal life, else your partner ends up with an extramarital affair with your neighbour. (trust me, i experienced this as a neighbour)

6* Feel good, the ability to feel good is a skill .you can feel good anytime, the question is are you actually willing to make it happen ??

7* In my personal opinion, every person must write a journal, it helps you to learn. observe & correct your mistakes.

8* Listening to 1 ted talk daily (you can do it during travelling too not now due to corona)

9* Become a member of 5 AM CLUB and don't forget to add workout & meditation (trust me, you'll notice miracle soon)

Every day recall " what is your ultimate goal in life? planning the most important thing but most of us don't do it.

10* " IF you fail to plan, you're planning to fail – BENJAMIN FRANKLIN.

11* BE nice, if you see someone who looks down, compliment them on something, their shoe, hair etc.. make sure that should be genuine. you will immediately notice the power of "genuine compliment " (personally tried)

12* Multi work is just a myth, you can do one work at a time in a good way, so focus on it wisely & save time & enjoy that work...

13* TAKE THE RISKS. Just drive out the fear of your failure, trust me this would be the 1st step of your success.

14* Explore more places. you'll notice plenty of things to learn, just travel as much as you can. meet new people, learn new things.

15* it's your time MAN. AFTER work it's time for yourself, do what makes you energetic & happy. Bring that child in yourself, which you lost years ago because of "LOG KYA KAHENGE " FUCK THIS THING AND FLY AS YOU CAN BECAUSE THERE IS NO ANOTHER YOU IN THIS UNIVERSE.

16* Visit a village/ farmhouse once in a while. just find a day and go to the countryside, watch people, birds chirping & temple bells ringing. witness the love, joy & affection, you'll love & learn many things.

17* Don't seek motivation, motivation is just a myth.

18* Dress Well, you can't underestimate the power of well dressing. so dress like you're going to meet a beloved one..

19* KEEP A GRATITUDE JOURNAL. this will help you get a sense of being thankful to the supreme power god, to the people around you and also about who is reading this, of course, I'm talking about you..

20* you live once is wrong ,you live everyday , so make it awesome every day but you die once , thats not wrong

LAST BUT NOT LEAST, YOU ARE UNIQUE & AWESOME , KEEP GROWING &

CHAPTER THREE

1. The majority of people will care about you, only if they've something to gain.

2. kindness is the ultimate beauty

3. Never share your weakness with your friends & even think twice before sharing with loved ones, people will consider you an easy target & take advantage of your weakness.

4. In life, nobody cares about your dream. nobody sees life exactly as you do, no one looks exactly like you on earth, so remember if you fail, you only have yourself to blame. you are responsible for your own destiny.

5. Sex is very important for a happy life.

6. masturbation is not a replacement for sex.

7. Each & Every person is partially based on his sensibilities & persona.

8. One day you'll die & no one gives a shit about you.

9. Most humans are most dangerous & canning when it comes to money matters.

10. Drinking done occasionally is a real stress buster.

11. Life is bitch & will f**k you in every hole if you don't give enough importance to it.

12. Exercise is not meant to have a healthy body, but it also helps in having a sound brain, without exercise your mind will be lazy too, Tim Cook, Mark Zuckerberg, bill gates exercise daily yet they don't have 6 pack abs, get that point ??

13. Waking up early won't do you much good if you don't manage your time wisely.

14. Before lending money to someone ask yourself 2 questions

(A):- Do I trust this person that he'll pay me back?

(B):- Can I afford to lose this money I am lending?

If the answer is no for any of the questions above, don't lend it..

15. Either look or bank balance both are important.

RICH SAYS:- MONEY DOESN'T MATTER

BEAUTIFUL SAYS:- LOOK DOESN'T MATTER

BUT ASK THE VICTIM WHO SUFFERED.

16. IF you think something is ugly, look harder. ugliness is just a failure of seeing.

17. Pleasure during sexx is two way street.

18. The only person you are answerable to is "YOURSELF"

19. Those who are in relationship will tell you " Relationship are great " & those who going through breakup will tell you " Relationship are toxic " don't listen to anyone , cut the crap & experience yourself.

20. Your parents are not right every time, sometimes they more care about fucking society , & their pride so use your own mind for future decisions.

21. Smoking & drinking are bad for health but very helpful if you are seeking good friendship in any workplace.

22. Initially ,A female offers her body in return for love n care & male loves women in return for sexxual satisfaction (mutual transaction) *talking about majority.

CHAPTER FOUR

The journey of an awesome life...

1. If the crowd goes one way, walk the other way.

2. Read a book every week. Not just fiction, but also non-fiction, self-help, fantasy, philosophy, metaphysics, psychology.

3. Open your mind to a new genre of books every 2 months and force yourself to read the best in that genre. If you like the book, pick up similar books and read.

4. Watch one critically acclaimed movie every week. Not just Hollywood, but also French, German, Indian, Australian, British, Japanese, Chinese, Korean, etc.

5. Open your mind to new genres of movies and movies from different countries every 2 months.

6. Lift weights and do resistance training at least 4 times a week.

7. Try to stop eating any food with a commercial.

8. Look at the ingredients before you buy something (for instance, Nutella has almost 60-70% sugar, the jam has around 48% sugar, and so on). Be informed about what you feed your body.

9. Don't listen to the people who say "this is the age to eat" when you're in your teens and twenties. You can eat anything at any age if you build your lifestyle around training your body well and eating healthy, nutritious food.

10. If someone says you can't do something, and you want to do it (whether you think you can or can't), go ahead and do it. Go ahead and have all the pleasure of proving them wrong. (No sweeter

pleasure on planet earth).

11. Sleep naked.

12. Cuddle with your beloved naked.

13. Embrace your body as a whole. Don't slice it into different parts and address some parts with pride and some parts with shame.

14. Embrace your life as a whole. Don't slice it into different parts (of the present, past, and future) and stop addressing some parts of your life with pride and some with shame (even if shame is what you feel about all of it).

15. Stop constructing your body to the standard of beauty set by people around you. Set your own standard. Get fat if you want. Get fit if you want. Get shredded if you want. Get muscular if you want. Squat regularly and get a big round butt if that's what you want. Make sure you're ready to face the consequences of whatever you choose to pursue after deciding you want it (getting fat doesn't come with that many good consequences). On the whole, stop living up to the standards other people set for you. Start setting your own standards for yourself.

16. Don't respect someone because they're elder to you. Stupid people get older too. Respect human beings in general, regardless of age – that's basic courtesy. Anything beyond that must come from a place of humility, empathy, and acceptance.

17. If you're married (or if you're in a relationship), it doesn't matter where you get your appetite, as long as you go home to eat.

18. Sometimes you can't have it all. Deal with it or go broke.

19. Sometimes you can't do it all. Do what you do best or see yourself failing trying to do everything at once.

20. Sometimes – not having it all, not doing it all – have to do with situations where you are not the only one involved – mostly relationships. If it ain't making you both happy, leave.

21. Do something you love, for at least 2 hours every day.

22. Have a "no-technology" time from 4 hours before you go to bed. No phones, no social media, no computers, no TV, nothing else. Just you, probably books, or probably your friends/family/

spouse/children, and just talk, eat, drink, and rejoice.

23. Drink in moderation. Preferably, stop drinking.

24. Don't even think about smoking in moderation. NEVER smoke. Don't pick it up even when a stupid so-called "friend" dares you to. It's better "not to try" some things even for once in a lifetime. (some rules you can break sometimes, like me)

25. Walk around in nature at least twice a week for one hour each time.

26. Say thanks to your food for nourishing you, before you eat it.

27. Reserve 4 hours for complete radio silence one day per week. In those 4 hours, go to a serene and peaceful place – in your home, or somewhere outside, and sit silently – observe everything that's going on – both inside as well as outside.

28. Take a lot of pictures.

29. Watch a stand-up comedy, preferably half an hour every day.

30. Learn an instrument that's not too mainstream, like Cello, Clarinet, Saxophone, Mandolin, bluegrass guitar, etc. Doing this will rewire your brain, and at least an hour of practice every day will make you feel peaceful, at ease, and excited to go about your work for the rest of the day. Over the years, as you master the instrument, you'll also see your sense of self-worth rising, your brain-stretching, and you'll realize you can do just about anything if you persist!

31. Teach the instrument, once you learn. Pass it on.

32. Go to an orphanage or a children's hospital at least once in two months. Talk to them. Listen to their stories. Get some help for them if you can, then you will realise what is the meaning of life..

33. Tell people you love, you love them.

34. More importantly, show people you love that you love them.

35. Don't take anyone for granted.

36. If someone isn't valuing you the way you know you deserve to be valued, walk away.

37. If you're an option in someone who's a priority to you, un-prioritize them.

38. Don't play games with someone's feelings. Be straightforward about how you feel.

39. If you know someone's manipulating you, either walk away or confront them.

40. If you know someone's been giving their all for you, with very little in return from you, go out of your way to show them that you care, that you know what it means.

41. Minimise the amount of technology you have.

42. Get a USB hub.

43. If you haven't worn something for over a year, give it away.

44. Don't buy anything if it is not immediately necessary or urgently needed. Simply put, don't buy anything for luxury.

45. Sponsor a girl child's education from kindergarten until she finishes college.

46. If you're a man, shave every day, and cut your hair once in three months. Refer to point 15, if you don't like this advice.

47. If you're a woman, you know what to do.

48. Drink a gallon of water every day.

49. Kill your television.

50. Cook with Garlic.

51. Write down your blessings and what you're grateful for, every day before you begin the day. just give a try for 2 weeks only, trust me .you will thank me later

52. Assume the best by default – in people, situations, and things. (With dogs, you don't even have to assume).

53. Get a dog (or a cat if you prefer cats).

54. Go on a road trip once in 6 months at the least. Brownie points for road-tripping somewhere you have never even remotely been to, in your life.

55. Swallow your pride and ask for help, if you can't do it all by yourself.

56. Swallow your pride and let other people help you if they offer to.

57. Read poetry. You'll learn to see the beauty in the simplest of things.

58. Don't take yourself too seriously. Don't take yourself too lightly either. Maintain a balance of self-deprecating humour, and

self-accepting pride.

59. Put on a crazy-ass song, dance like it's your last day. Feel yourself getting high on the dance and the music.

60. Put on karaoke and sing on top of your voice. Sing out loud.

61. Cry. Cry out loud. Get it all out.

62. Laugh. Laugh out loud. Laugh as much as you can. Laugh as long as you want to.

63. Cook for yourself twice a month. Whatever you want, pull a recipe, plan beforehand, get the required groceries on the day prior, make them ready, get up early, start cooking. (A nice jazz or classical background music would top it all!)

64. Stay away from 'Normal'.

65. Delete the assholes from your life – even if it is someone in the family.

66. Drink a shot of red wine after dinner (50ml). (indian don't try)

67. Call your parents at least once a week.

68. Visit them at least once a month.

69. Stay unplugged and disconnected from the society for at least 1 week every 6 months (while 1 week every 2 months would be awesome). How? Probably go camping without any technology or gadgets with you. Eat, sleep, make out, make love, read stories, read books (not kindle, actual books!), tell stories, make up stories, talk about the universe, talk about time-travel, talk about aliens, talk about sex, talk about interstellar, talk about anything, cuddle up, make out again, sleep, wake up again, watch the stars, make a wish on a falling star, do something impulsive, explore each other, or just explore your inner-self (if you're alone).

70. Don't be a doormat.

71. Observe more than you expose.

72. Give to yourself before you give to others (mainly love).

73. When you give to others, give unconditionally.

74. Don't lend money, especially to friends. If you're gonna give money to friends, consider it as a gift you give to your friend. Otherwise, you'll lose your friend more often than not.

75. Speak good things about anyone you speak of. Filter out the bad things.

76. Take only the good things when others talk about someone else. Filter out the bad things.

77. Stop hanging out around the "complainers" – those who always have something to complain about.

78. Stop posting statuses indirectly for someone on whatsapp or facebook. If you have the guts, tell them directly. Otherwise, do away with it. Don't be stupid.

79. Stop discussing your problems. Most people are glad you have them. The rest just don't care. There's no point. Either deal with it, or just stop worrying.

79. Stop discussing your goals. Most people won't help you with your goals when you need something. Some people get jealous. The rest don't even care.

80. Cry as much as you want. But make sure that's the last time you cry for whatever you're crying for.

81. Laugh as much as you want. But make sure that's not the last time you laugh about what you're laughing about.

82. Once a week, don't look at the clock for an entire day. Just do what you love or what you want to do.

83. Leave the country if you're not happy here.

84. Stop watching porn. Start going out – if you're single. Explore tantra – if you're in a relationship.

85. Let your children play. Let your kids be kids. Give them a vast canvas for them to paint in – both literally, and metaphorically.

86. Listen to a different genre of music every month. Open your mind to different genres and force yourself to listen to them for one month or until you want to explore more. If you don't like it even after one month, stop. If you love it after one month or even before that, explore more of that genre.

87. Start journaling – your day's life, and your night's dreams. Keep a separate journal for writing about the dreams you get while asleep, write them as soon as you're awake, as much as you can remember. Slowly you'll develop lucidity, and you can even explore

lucid dreams, astral projection, etc.

88. Talk to people who aren't like you – people with an opposite mindset, opposite lifestyle, etc. Learn what makes them tick.

89. Love him/her like he/she can be taken away from you any moment now.

90. Treat him/her like he/she is gonna be with you until the end of your universe.

91. Put 50% of your income away in savings before you spend on anything.

92. Once a month, indulge in a DIY activity, a project of sorts, and involve everyone in your family – your kids, wife, yourself, parents, and anyone in your family who's present at your home that day. Rejoice, eat well, dine fine, drink wine, sing karaoke, tell stories, at the end of the day, as the mark of celebrating the completion of the project.

93. Go and play outside with your kids. If you're a kid, just go and play outside.

94. Soak in the sweat, enjoy the summer, dance in the rain, enjoy the shower, with a cup of tea and book by the windowsill, enjoy the winter!

95. Be present in the moment. Don't wish for something in the future now – you'll wish for something else there in the future when you have what you want for the future now. So, start practising relishing the moment, while working for what you want. You'll always be happy.

96. Be grateful for what you have. Most people don't have what you have.

97. Be grateful also for what you don't have. Most people suffer by having what you don't have – either directly or indirectly.

98. Spend time not money on your kids.

99. Spend time and money equally on your wife.

100. Always give your best in anything you do.

101. Always do more than you intended to.

LET'S SMILE TOGETHER

:)

1. Problems will come, This is certain, you cannot do anything about this JUST CHANGE APPROACH.

2. You cannot feel Happy always, there will be mood swings, happy times, bad times. This is natural, accept it.

3. Challenges makes us strong. The more we confront problems, the more we grow.

4. Worry habit drains energy. It's something natural we do in our free time. Either clinging from the past or thinking of the future.

5. Give F**k to things that are important. Not everything in this world requires your attention

.6. The magnitude of success depends on how many times you have failed. If someone is good this means he confronted failures more than you did.

7. You are not special. Nobody is watching us, actually, nobody cares. People are busy in themselves thinking about their own shit. So chill

.8. Everyone wants a reward but not a struggle. We want success but not setbacks, we want to be leaders but do not want to stretch our limits, we want to be winners but we don't want to go through rigorous pain. Enjoy the path, success is just a state of mind.

9. You will die one day This is inevitable. Accept this and be a Messenger of love. Spread love, live life, Keep a smile on.

Most important

10 . Sometimes we get confused in situations, unable to decide what to do next. Whether it's the preparation for an exam or any important decision in life, we think from where to start. To CONQUER THE CONFUSED STATE OF MIND IS DO SOMETHING, Don't sit ideal.

SEE YOU SOON :)

CONNECT WITH ME :- lifestyle_read_travel_blogger (INSTAGRAM)

HAVE SUGGESTIONS ? : nkkrishna01@gmail.com